MUMMIES
OF THE PHARAOHS
Exploring the
Valley of the Kings

MELVIN BERGER & GILDA BERGER

SCHOLASTIC INC.
New York Toronto London Auckland Sydney
Mexico City New Delhi Hong Kong Buenos Aires

ISBN 0-439-33595-7

12 11 10 9 8   5 6/0

Printed in the U.S.A.   **24**

First Scholastic printing, October 2001

PUBLISHED BY
THE NATIONAL GEOGRAPHIC SOCIETY

John M. Fahey, Jr.
President and Chief Executive Officer

Gilbert H. Grosvenor
Chairman of the Board

Nina D. Hoffman
Senior Vice President

PREPARED BY
THE BOOK DIVISION

William R. Gray
Vice President and Director

Charles Kogod
Assistant Director

Barbara A. Payne
Editorial Director and Managing Editor

Note: The dates, names, and spellings used in this book are based on the research of Rolf Krauss of the Egyptian Museum in Berlin, Germany.

Front Cover: The mummy of Ramses II.

Title Page: The head of a gold-sheathed fan found in King Tutankhamun's tomb. The curved edge once held ostrich feathers. A similar fan appears at the very left in the illustration on the fan.

Contents Page: A golden leopard-head clasp, found in King Tutankhamun's tomb, held a leopard-skin cloak in place.

Page 5: The inner coffin of King Tutankhamun.

Back Cover: A portion of the golden mask that covered King Tutankhamun's face under all his burial wrappings.

STAFF FOR THIS BOOK

Nancy Laties Feresten
Director of Children's Publishing

Suzanne Patrick Fonda
Editor

Jennifer Emmett
Associate Editor

Jo Tunstall
Assistant Editor, Project Editor, and Illustrations Research

Marianne Koszorus
Design Director of Children's Publishing

David Seager
Book Designer

John Agnone
Illustrations Editor

Sharon Berry
Illustrations Assistant

Carl Mehler
Director of Maps

Joseph F. Ochlak
Map Research

Jerome N. Cookson
Map Production

Anne Marie Houppert
Indexer

R. Gary Colbert
Production Director

Lewis R. Bassford
Production Manager

Vincent P. Ryan
Manufacturing Manager

ILLUSTRATION CREDITS

Cover & back cover, Kenneth Garrett; 1, EMC/Fred J. Maroon; 3, Photo Archive; 4, James L. Stanfield; 6-7, Kenneth Garrett; 8-9, MMA; 10, Griffith Institute/James A. Sugar; 12, The Times Newspaper; 12-13, Photo Archive; 14 (both), Robert Harding Picture Library; 15 (le) EMC/Lee Boltin; 15 (top), Robert Harding Picture Library; 15 (ctr), EMC/Victor Boswell; (bot), Robert Harding Picture Library; 16-17, Robert Harding Picture Library; 18, EMC/Fred J. Maroon; 19, Photography by Egyptian Expedition, MMA; 20, Photography by Egyptian Expedition, MMA; 21, EMC/Victor Boswell; 22, Griffith Institute; 22-23, Kenneth Garrett; 24-25 (both), Griffith Institute; 26-27 (both) Robert Harding Picture Library; 28-29, O. Louis Mazzatenta; 31, EMC/Victor Boswell; 32, Bettmann/Corbis; 32-33, Farrell Grehan; 34-35, Kenneth Garrett; 36 (both), EMC/Victor Boswell; 38-39, Courtesy of the Oriental Institute of the University of Chicago; 39, Agyptisches Museum Berlin/Victor Boswell; 40-41, Kenneth Garrett; 42-43, The British Museum; 43, Farrell Grehan; 44-45 (both), Farrell Grehan; 46-47, Kenneth Garrett; 47, David Fierstein; 48, EMC/Victor Boswell; 49, Kenneth Garrett; 50-51 (both), Kenneth Garrett; 52, Christopher Klein; 53, Agyptisches Museum Berlin/Victor Boswell; 54-55, Christopher Klein; (insets) David Fierstein; 56-57, Kenneth Garrett; 58-59 (both), Victor Boswell; 60-61, Fotomas Index UK/Gordon Roberton; 62-63, Agyptisches Museum Berlin/Victor Boswell

EMC-The Egyptian Museum in Cairo
MMA-The Metropolitan Museum of Art

CONTENTS

INTRODUCTION

What does the title *Mummies of the Pharaohs* bring to mind? Many people think "pyramids." But did you know that the mummies of some of the most famous and fascinating pharaohs are not buried in the pyramids at all? Their tombs were built into the cliffs of the Valley of the Kings, nearly 500 miles south of the Great Pyramid of Giza.

The Egyptians stopped building pyramids as tombs for their pharaohs at the start of the New Kingdom, which lasted from 1539 B.C. to 1078 B.C., and instead started to create burial places in the Valley of the Kings. During this time, the pharaohs won many great battles against foreign forces, making Egypt the strongest and wealthiest nation in the world. Thebes, their capital, became the country's most important city—and the victorious rulers wanted to be buried near this center.

How do we know all this? Much information about ancient Egypt comes from Egyptologists, experts in the field, who excavate tombs and other sites. The paintings, writings, jewelry, furniture, and mummies they find reveal much about the rich civilization that existed in ancient Egypt.

This book tells the story of the Valley of the Kings and of some of the pharaohs who were buried there more than 3,000 years ago. We first join the search for the hidden tomb of King Tutankhamun. The discovery of his tomb in 1922 gave the modern world its most complete picture of life and death in Egypt's New Kingdom.

Then we travel back to the times of the pharaohs themselves and find out why Thutmosis I built the first tomb in the valley and what happened to some of the other rulers buried there. Finally, we learn about the making of Pharaoh Seti I's huge, ornate tomb, the preparations of his body for burial, and the funeral rituals.

The ancient Egyptians believed that to speak the names of the dead is to make them live again. And they were right. The magnificent and mysterious tombs of the Valley of the Kings still speak to us today. We hope you enjoy the stories they have to tell.

TWO ENGLISHMEN & A PHARAOH

It was a warm spring day in the year 1917. Two Englishmen rode donkey-back into the silent, dried-up river bed in Egypt called the Valley of the Kings. In the lead was the athletic, well-tanned Howard Carter, an expert on ancient Egypt. With him was the older, more portly, and very wealthy Lord Carnarvon. The men paused a moment, awestruck, before entering the small, barren valley where many of the kings, or pharaohs, of ancient Egypt were buried.

In his pocket, Carter had a large map of the valley. It showed a stretch of land on the west bank of the Nile River across from the city of Thebes (now called Luxor). More than 3,000 years ago, Egyptians cut dozens of tombs into the valley's rocky cliffs for their pharaohs.

Over the years, many of the tombs had been found and explored. But not the tomb of King Tutankhamun (TOOT-ahnk-ah-mun), sometimes shortened to King Tut, who reigned from 1333 to 1323 B.C. Lord Carnarvon and Howard Carter had come from London, England, to seek this pharaoh's tomb. Inside, the explorers hoped to find the king's mummy, along with priceless golden treasures. According to ancient Egyptian belief, the tomb would contain everything the dead ruler needed for a happy life in the next world, called the afterlife or the underworld.

Many mummies of the pharaohs were buried in the dry, barren Valley of the Kings. A mountain peak shaped like a pyramid overlooks the valley. The dark spot in the picture is the shadow

Carnarvon and Carter set up camp. Then, with a team of Egyptians, they began their search for Tutankhamun's final resting place. For many years, Carter had been exploring the Valley of the Kings and had already found several tombs. He had places in mind where they should look.

The rugged band of workers dug into the rocks and sand of the valley. With shovels, picks, and bare hands, the sweating crew hauled away tons of rubble.

For five years, the two Englishmen and their crew continued the quest. Patch by patch, they explored most of the valley. But they found nothing. Carter remained certain that Tutankhamun's tomb was still to be found. But Lord Carnarvon began to lose hope. Still, he agreed to give Carter money enough to hunt for one more year.

In 1922, Carter returned alone to Egypt. He and his men started to dig in a new place in the valley. Day after day they labored in the brutal heat, finding nothing more than a few old oil jars.

Then one afternoon, a young worker kicked some rocks away to make a flat place to set down his water jar. His heel struck something hard and sharp. He cried out and other workers rushed over. In no time, they uncovered a creamy white step, then another. Were these steps the entrance to a tomb?

Carter's men struggled to clear the steps, which led down to a plastered doorway. Carter examined the seal stamped into the plaster. It showed a jackal and nine captives, which Carter recognized as an official seal. But instead of entering, Carter covered up the staircase to hide

The entrance to King Tut's tomb is at the bottom of the photograph. The larger tomb above was for Ramses V. Although King Tut's tomb entrance is easy to see today, Howard Carter, Lord Carnarvon, and a large crew searched for five years before finding it in 1922.

the tomb entrance and sent a telegram to Carnarvon in England to hurry to Egypt at once.

When Lord Carnarvon arrived with his daughter, Lady Evelyn, Carter ordered his workers to clear the steps and uncover the base of the tomb door. Stooping over, Carter could see the markings at the bottom of the door. Painstakingly, he deciphered the name—Tutankhamun! Now Carter's crew began to break down the stone doorway, block by block. Behind the ancient wall, they discovered a long, sloping passageway. It was filled with rubble. Working feverishly, the laborers shoveled the broken rocks into baskets. Others carted the heavy loads out of the tomb.

At one point, a worker's shovel hit wood instead of stone. Carter dropped to the ground to view the object. It was a painted wooden head of young Tutankhamun rising out of a lotus flower. The men cheered. There could be little doubt. They were on the brink of a major discovery.

As soon as workers cleared a path through the passage, Carter and Carnarvon crawled through. At the far end was a second plaster-covered doorway stamped with the priests' seals. Using an iron rod, Carter chipped a hole in the door. A puff of stale, warm, 3,000-year-old air escaped from the room on the other side.

Trembling with excitement, Carter thrust a candle through the hole and peeked in. In the flickering light, he saw "...strange animals, statues, and gold—everywhere the glint of gold." There were gilded statues, chariots,

An iron gate now blocks the way to the room at the end of the passage into King Tut's tomb. Standing here, Carter, Lord Carnarvon, and Lady Evelyn first glimpsed the tomb's incredible treasures and riches, including three beds with sides shaped like lions, cows, and crocodiles. Some experts think King Tut may have been laid out on one of these beds while he was being mummified.

a throne, couches, shields and swords, musical instruments, model boats, chests, and much, much more.

In a few minutes Carter widened the hole and the group stepped through and into the room now known as the antechamber. Overcome by joy and excitement, they could hardly breathe. It was indeed the treasure-filled tomb of the Pharaoh Tutankhamun!

While exploring the chamber, Lord Carnarvon spied a hole in the wall behind one of the couches. Peering through it, he could see another room with a jumble of precious boxes, baskets, stools, chairs, beds, and other household goods. It was treasure beyond imagining.

A worker carrying a life-size wooden torso of King Tut (above) walks behind Howard Carter. Tailors may have used the dummy to help fit the king's clothes. Holding a flashlight to a hole in the doorway, the awestruck Carter surveyed this scene (right). Against the wall were gilt beds. A chest of linen clothes rested on one bed. A throne stood beneath it. Four dismantled chariots were piled nearby.

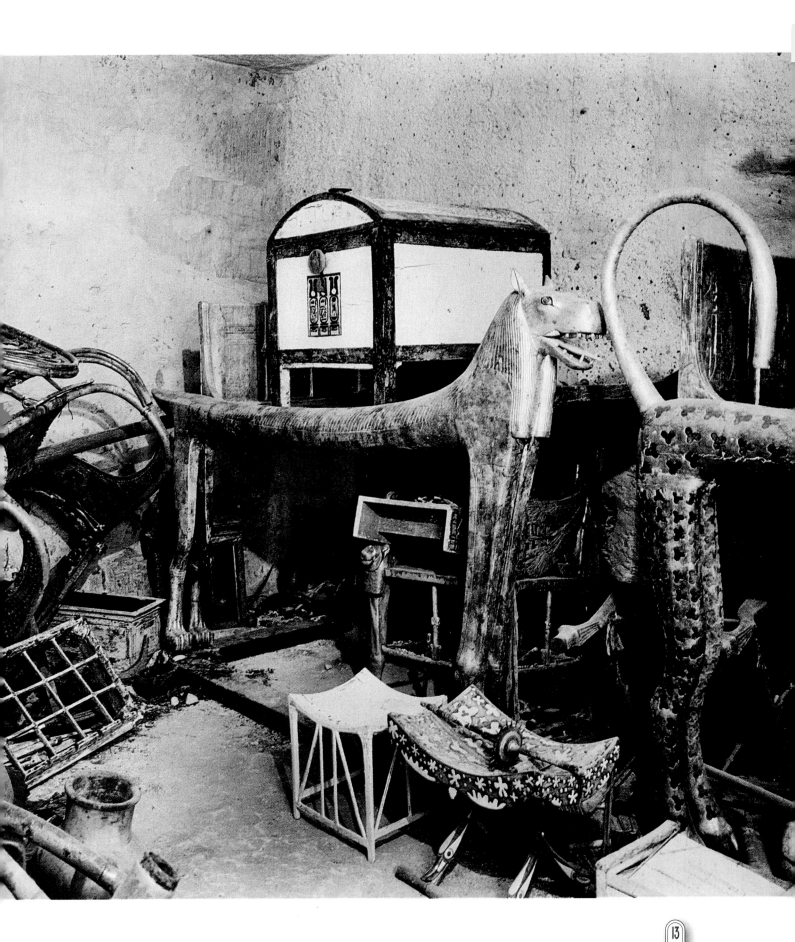

TREASURES FROM KING TUTANKHAMUN'S TOMB

Carter, Lord Carnarvon, and Lady Evelyn glimpsed a treasure trove of stunning objects when they entered King Tut's tomb for the first time in mid-afternoon, November 26, 1922. The glint of gold and the incredible abundance of items in the room dazzled their eyes.

Carter found evidence that twice burglars had broken into the tomb in the distant past, but he guessed that both times they had been caught and were not able to haul away their loot. Government officials probably resealed the door to the tomb each time. With its remarkable mummy

and the priceless items it contained, King Tut's tomb gave the world a view into the life and burial practices of pharaohs 3,000 years ago. This small sample of the tomb's contents gives a clue to its great riches.

This scene, from the gold-covered throne at left, shows Queen Ankhesenamun rubbing an ointment on her husband, King Tutankhamun. The sun's rays, with hands at the ends, illuminate the couple.

King Tut slept with his head on this blue glass headrest.

The inner soles of King Tut's sandals pictured Egypt's enemies. The King symbolically crushed them each time he took a step.

According to ancient Egyptian belief, a gold-covered cobra amulet, or charm, would help the pharaoh pass safely through the underworld.

Inside this wooden chest covered with colorful hunting and battle scenes, Carter found the headrest and sandals as well as a robe that belonged to King Tut.

Meantime, Lady Evelyn, left behind in the first chamber, approached two life-size statues. Dressed in gold skirts, sandals, and headdresses, they appeared to be guarding something. Their hands held maces and staffs, as if ready to slay anyone who tried to pass. Running her hands along the wall between the figures, Lady Evelyn could make out the outline of still another doorway. Greatly elated, she called Carter over.

Carter longed to explore the sealed room—but did not. He wanted the three of them to be alone when they inspected the chamber for the first time. Pretending he wasn't interested, Carter led everybody away from the tomb.

The next night around midnight, without telling anyone, the three companions returned to the site by themselves. Quietly, they crept down the steps into the passageway and entered the antechamber. Carter hacked open a passageway in the hidden doorway between the two statues. Squeezing through on all fours, Carter, Carnarvon, and Evelyn ventured into the tomb's main room, the burial chamber. Perspiring from the heat and shivering with anticipation, the group stood speechless before a dazzling blue and gold shrine. Such a shrine, which was usually a highly decorated, generally room-sized box that holds a mummy or other object of high regard, was commonly used in the burial of a pharaoh.

Two golden doors on the shrine, held shut by two black bolts, blocked their way further into the burial chamber. Carter was extremely eager to enter the shrine. But he knew there was other work to be done first. He had to list, draw or photograph, and remove all the objects in the

King Tut and his wife are shown on a golden panel.
The hieroglyphs around the couple give their names and titles.

antechamber and its annex. This took months.

Finally, Carter stood once again before the two golden doors. He pulled back the black bolts. As he tugged gently, the two huge doors slowly swung open. Inside was another shrine, the doors securely tied with heavy rope. The knot had not been touched since the priests burying Tutankhamun had fastened it thousands of years before.

Carter carefully cut the cord. The doors opened. They revealed a third shrine, and then a fourth. Carter drew back the last doors.

Within stood a huge golden yellow stone sarcophagus. It was beautifully carved and decorated. Carter passed his hand lovingly over the heavy lid. But even as he breathed a deep sigh of pleasure, he realized how much more work remained to be done.

In April 1923, four months after finding King Tut's tomb, Lord Carnarvon died. But with financial help from Lady

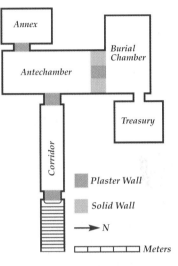

Plan of Tutankhamun's tomb. The contents included furniture, foods, chariots, couches, statues, religious items, King Tut's mummy, its shrines, and much more.

The golden shrine doors at the left are very much like the doors that blocked the way to the other shrines around the mummy of King Tut. A knot of heavy rope (above), which the priests had tied more than 3,000 years before, held together the doors to the second shrine.

Evelyn, Carter was able to carry on. Because of the work involved in recording and removing objects, it took more than a year before Carter was ready to raise the heavy stone lid on the sarcophagus. Inside, he found a magnificent coffin that surpassed all his imaginings. The coffin was in the shape of a mummified body and covered in gold. In fact, it was so large, Carter guessed there must be more coffins inside it. And so there were.

Carter (above), having opened the door to the second shrine, gazes in wonder at the third. The massive stone sarcophagus (right) held King Tut's magnificent nested coffins.

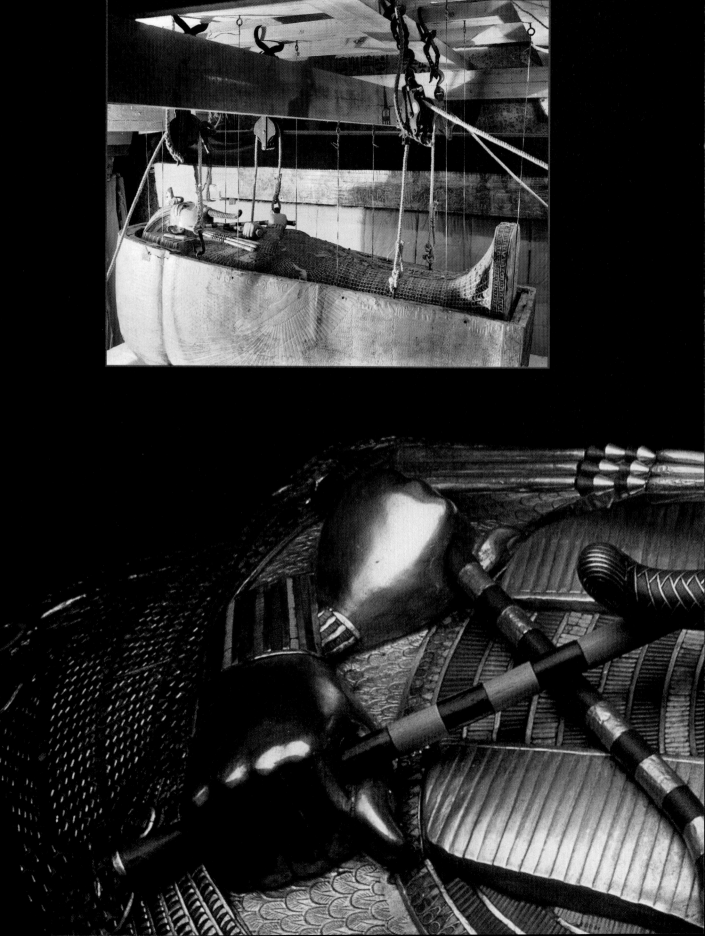

Carter found two more coffins nestled within the first, each more magnificent than the one above. The innermost coffin, which was of solid gold, was the most richly decorated of all. Inside lay the king's mummy, wrapped in linen bandages held together with gold bands. Inscribed on the bands was a wish for the pharaoh's safe journey to the next world.

With utmost care, Carter removed the gold mask from the mummy's head. As he gazed at the young pharaoh, Carter asked himself: How had the young king died at only eighteen years of age?

Having removed the lid of the outer coffin (left), Carter is about to take out the second coffin. The top of the solid-gold inner coffin (below) shows King Tut holding the farmer's flail and the shepherd's crook — symbols of both divinity and royalty. The massive inner coffin weighed over a ton.

Carter suspected that Tut was buried in a tomb not intended for him—or for any other royal figure. The tomb seemed too small for a king. The wall paintings were overly simple and appeared unfit for royalty. The burial shrines were hastily and clumsily put together. The sarcophagus lid was cracked. And even the faces on the coffins did not look alike.

Was this because Tut died so young that there had not been enough time to prepare a proper tomb? Or was his burial rushed before anyone could investigate his death? Howard Carter never could explain why Tutankhamun died at such an early age. But since then, x-rays of the mummy's skull have given valuable clues. They show that Tutankhamun received a blow to his head—hard enough to kill.

Tutankhamun's mummified head (left) shows signs of a powerful blow to the base of his skull that has not yet been explained. Before the priests wrapped King Tut's mummy in linen, they capped his toes with gold and placed gold sandals on his feet (right).

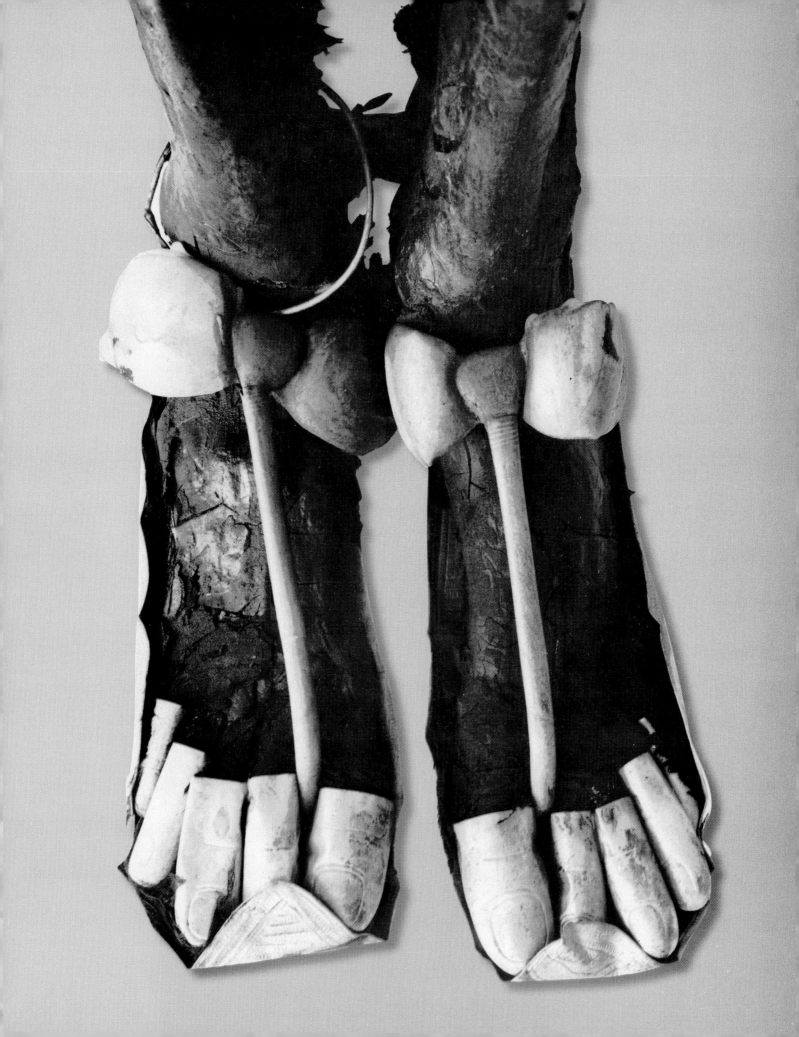

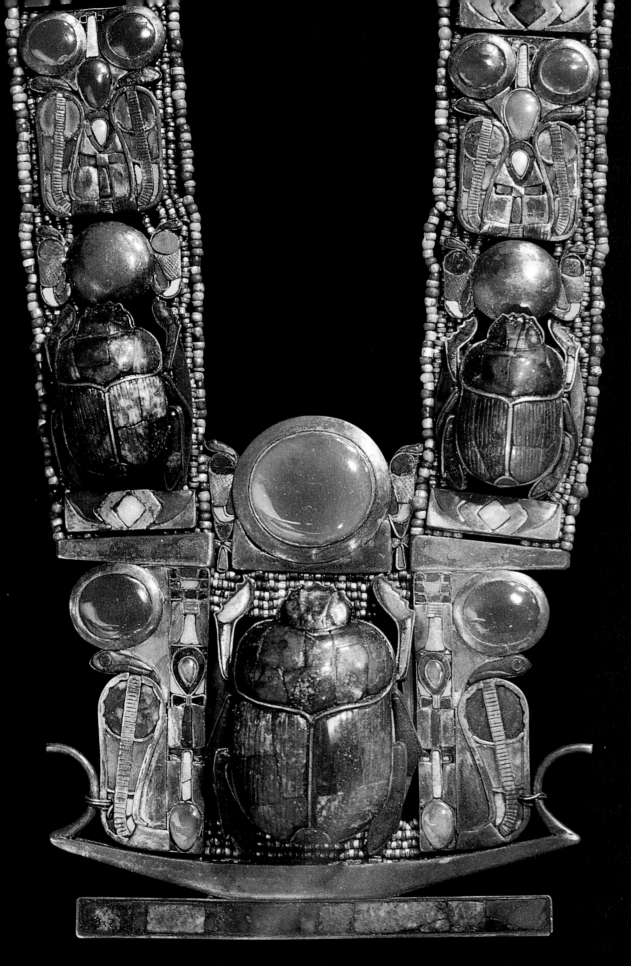

If it was murder, the most likely suspect is an advisor named Ay. He was one of the two men assigned to rule with Tutankhamun when the boy became pharaoh at the age of nine. Ay had a motive, for he succeeded in becoming pharaoh himself shortly after the young man's death.

Finding the intact tomb of Tutankhamun exceeded all expectations. It was the first royal burial place in the Valley of the Kings that had not been emptied by grave robbers. King Tutankhamun's mummy, the magnificent riches, paintings, statues, and objects of daily life revealed much about Egypt during the period of the New Kingdom.

The center and sides of King Tut's necklace depict sacred scarabs (left). These beetles are symbols of life after death. This heavy earring (right) belonged to the king. His mummy (page 24) shows a large, pierced hole in the earlobe.

GRAVE MYSTERIES

Thutmosis I became pharaoh of Egypt in the year 1493 B.C., near the beginning of the New Kingdom and almost 160 years before King Tut. Like other pharaohs, he began to think about his burial soon after he took office. But, unlike his ancestors, he chose to be buried in the Valley of the Kings. Why did he pick this new place?

Egyptologists think they know. For more than a thousand years before Thutmosis I, the Egyptians had buried most of their royalty in huge stone pyramids near such cities as Giza, Saqqara, and Dahshur. The structures were carefully designed to protect the mummified bodies and kingly treasures for the afterworld. But the pyramids had not kept out thieves and vandals.

Thutmosis thought that a tomb in the valley would be a safer burial place than a pyramid. The valley had only one narrow entrance. The king could post soldiers there to keep out robbers.

Like other Egyptians, Thutmosis worshiped the sun, among many other gods. Looking toward the west bank of the Nile, he saw the sun disappear behind the desert mountains every evening and believed that it entered the underworld. To be buried in the valley would mean eternal life in the underworld, enjoying the sun's light and warmth when it was not shining on Earth. (In fact, the Egyptian word for *to die* means *to go west*.)

The entrance to the tomb of Ramses II is filled with Egyptian writing called hieroglyphs. This wall praises the sun god in his more than 70 different forms. Today, gates block the entrances to all the graves of the pharaohs in the Valley of the Kings.

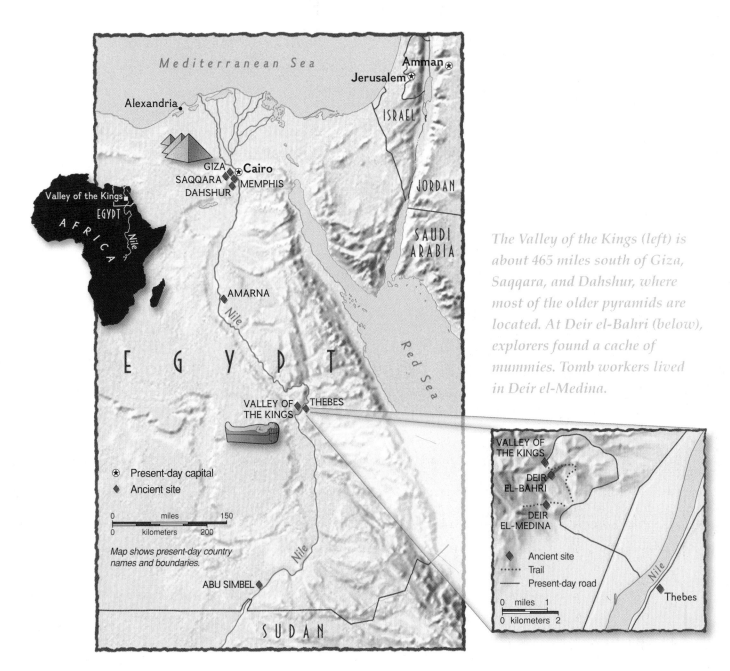

The Valley of the Kings (left) is about 465 miles south of Giza, Saqqara, and Dahshur, where most of the older pyramids are located. At Deir el-Bahri (below), explorers found a cache of mummies. Tomb workers lived in Deir el-Medina.

In addition, on the western bank of the Nile, a small mountain peak shaped like a pyramid overlooked the entire valley. In the Egyptian religion, the sloping sides of a pyramid represented the sun's slanting rays coming to Earth. This naturally occurring pyramid made the valley sacred ground.

Whatever his thinking, Thutmosis I ordered his architect, a man named Ineni, to draw up plans for a tomb in the valley. Ineni boasted that he dug the tomb in secret.

"I supervised the digging of the cliff tomb of His Majesty alone, no one seeing, no one hearing," he wrote. Of course, he failed to mention the dozens of people who did the actual work!

Ineni and his crew tunneled out the tomb now known as KV 20 (KV stands for King's Valley; the number is the order in which the tombs were discovered). Workers cut its entrance high in a cliff at the eastern edge of the valley, well hidden in a deep cleft in the rock. And here priests carefully interred the mummy of Thutmosis I after his death in 1483 B.C. But the body did not rest in peace.

After Thutmosis I died, his son Thutmosis II became pharaoh. And when he passed on, his child, Thutmosis III, ascended the throne, even though he was only 10 years old.

Officials asked Hatshepsut (hat-SHEP-soot), the boy's step-

Thutmosis III wears a head piece, false beard, and kilt to signify his position as pharaoh. Known as the Warrior Pharaoh, he conquered the lands of present-day Israel and Syria.

mother and daughter of Thutmosis I, to help Thutmosis III govern Egypt until he was old enough to rule alone. Instead, Hatshepsut proclaimed herself Pharaoh of Egypt and continued to rule long after Thutmosis III was old enough to take over. She reigned for 22 years, from 1479 to 1458 B.C. The queen organized trade expeditions and led armies in battle. Like male pharaohs, she sometimes appeared in public wearing a false beard as a way of commanding respect.

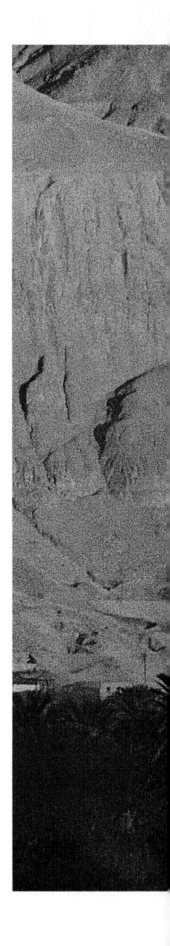

Thutmosis III was furious. He was especially annoyed that she planned to be buried in KV 20, the tomb of her father. She had added a large burial chamber to his tomb, with space enough for two coffins. When Queen Hatshepsut finally died, the priests carried out her wishes and buried her next to her father in KV 20.

Thutmosis took revenge. He had most statues of the queen smashed to bits and her name removed from temples and monuments. Even more important, he directed that another tomb be built, KV 38. Then he moved the mummy of his grandfather, Thutmosis I, from KV 20 to the newly dug KV 38—just to get him away from the much-hated Hatshepsut.

The life-size statue (above) represents Hatshepsut in the formal pose of a pharaoh, wearing the traditional pharaonic head piece. Hatshepsut's temple (right) stands in Deir el-Bahri, with the Valley of the Kings in the background.

THE VALLEY OF THE KINGS

Practically all the pharaohs of the New Kingdom were buried in the Valley of the Kings. The tombs were arranged randomly, some in remote locations, some almost on top of others. When Egyptologists began to explore the valley, they had no idea whose tomb was whose, so they gave each tomb a number. KV stood for King's Valley; the number, for the order in which the tomb was found.

So far, 62 tombs have been discovered in the valley. As you might guess, King Tutankhamun's is KV 62. Most tombs were built for pharaohs, but there were some for members of royal families, an occasional nobleman, and even treasured pets. Egyptologists do not expect to find any more tombs in the valley. But they have been saying that for 100 years!

KV 35

KV 14

KV 15   KV 38

KV 47

KV 57

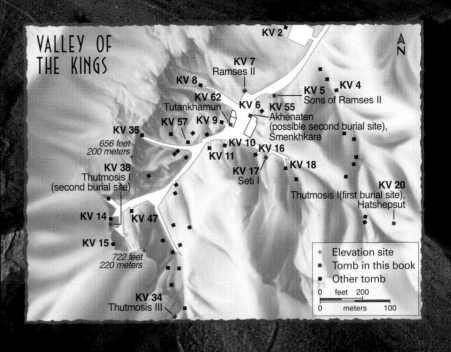

The many tombs, temples, shrines, and other ruins that blanket Thebes (now Luxor) and its surrounding area have kept Egyptologists busy here for nearly two centuries.

KV 8

KV 9

KV 7

KV 11

KV 62

KV 55

KV 6

KV 10

KV 5

KV 16

The mummy of Thutmosis I did not rest in peace here either. About 500 years later, Egyptian officials discovered that grave robbers had raided almost every tomb in the Valley of the Kings. To protect the rest, priests collected more than 40 royal mummies, including Thutmosis I, and hid them all in a mountain tomb a few miles from the Valley of the Kings in the area known as Deir el-Bahri.

This tomb, often called a cache, became Thutmosis I's third, and ultimate, resting place.

The carved limestone tablet from Akhenaten's tomb in Amarna portrays Akhenaten and his family worshiping Aten, the disk of the sun. In their hands they hold offerings for the god.

But at least we know where Thutmosis I is. The mummy of Pharaoh Akhenaten is still missing.

Akhenaten (ack-en-AH-ten) was born Amenhotep IV and ruled from 1353 to 1336 b.c. Although reputed to be gawky and deformed, the young pharaoh had great charm. Many think he was the most complex and extraordinary figure in the ancient world. He is certainly one of the most puzzling.

Before Amenhotep IV, Egyptians worshiped many gods and goddesses. Temples devoted to the various deities were found throughout the country. Huge numbers of priests conducted elaborate temple ceremonies and bestowed bountiful offerings on the statues.

The new pharaoh believed that the priests were becoming too rich and powerful. He rejected the idea of many gods and declared belief in only one god, Aten, the disk of the sun. And he demanded that the people give up their devotion to all other gods except Aten.

Like many other statues of Akhenaten, this one shows an unusual looking man. No one is sure why artists portrayed him this way. It may be that this is how he really looked or that such a depiction was just part of the new art style.

The painting (above), which shows two of Akhenaten's daughters in an affectionate pose, illustrates the warm, graceful, and informal new art style. In this family scene of Akhenaten and his beautiful wife Nefertiti (right), the two are in a garden, bathed by the rays of Aten, playing with three of their six daughters.

In an isolated spot about 250 miles downriver from Thebes, the pharaoh built a great new capital city dedicated to Aten. It was called Tel el-Amarna, or Amarna for short. At the same time, the pharaoh changed his name to Akhenaten, incorporating the god's name into his own.

Akhenaten's religious and social changes led to new approaches in painting and sculpture. The pharaoh's artists now used a fresh, livelier art style, quite different from the stiff formality of earlier times. Instead of unnatural poses, Akhenaten insisted that painters portray him looking casual and relaxed, with an arm around his wife's waist or lounging in the garden with a daughter on his knee.

Not everyone was happy with the many unusual practices that were sweeping the country. Priests and others secretly opposed Akhenaten's teachings. Even Akhenaten's most devoted followers were alarmed at his loss of authority. With the priests revolting and foreign enemies trying to take back lands the Egyptians had conquered, trouble was brewing both at home and abroad.

Akhenaten died when he was not more than 42 years of age and officials buried him in the tomb he had built for himself in Amarna.

After his death, the new rulers demanded the return of the former religion. They declared Akhenaten a heretic and ordered the destruction of Amarna. The pharaoh's followers, afraid that his enemies would destroy his mummy and damage his tomb, had his body moved to the Valley of the Kings for safety.

Most Egyptologists believed that Pharaoh Akhenaten's second resting place was KV 55. Recent evidence suggests, however, that the body in KV 55 is Smenkhkare, the pharaoh who ruled between Akhenaten and Tutankhamun.

In the tomb, though, researchers found a shrine for Akhenaten's mother, Queen Tiye, and a coffin and some jars with the name Kiya, one of Akhenaten's wives.

Explorers found the body of Ramses II in the cache at Deir el-Bahri that contained many other mummies. Workers removed the mummy from the tomb, unwrapped it, and placed it on the ground. According to an old story, the broiling sun caused the mummy's crossed arms to slowly separate and rise—leading many to think the pharaoh had come back to life.

Why were Queen Tiye's and Kiya's things found in tomb KV 55? And where is Akhenaten's mummy? His burial remains a mystery.

Ramses II was crowned pharaoh in 1279 and served until 1213 B.C. Nicknamed Ramses the Great for his triumphs in battle, this king of ancient Egypt had eight royal wives and an untold number of secondary wives. By all of them he had more than 100 children—a greater number than any other pharaoh. He also ruled Egypt for

Ramses II, seated at the right, receives tribute from the conquered land of Kush in Nubia (above). The gifts include live animals, leopard skins, elephant tusks, spears, shields, furniture, gold rings, and much more. The carving at the right shows the pharaoh on his chariot shooting arrows at his enemies as he charges into battle.

a record 66 years. Ramses II reached 90 years of age at a time when most Egyptians lived only about half as long.

During most of his long reign, Ramses II devoted himself to a vast building program along the Nile. Among his many projects was the construction of the biggest tomb in the Valley of the Kings—KV 5.

Explorers discovered KV 5 in the 1820s. They assigned it a number, but since the tomb was flooded with mud and debris, it was soon forgotten. Then, early in 1989, Egyptian authorities decided to widen a road into the Valley of the Kings. Believing that the road might pass over the entrance

Among the most spectacular buildings erected by Ramses II was his monumental Great Temple at Abu Simbel (above), many miles from the Valley of the Kings. The front of the temple originally had four huge, seated figures of Ramses—each some 67 feet high. A close-up of the head of one figure (left) gives a feeling for its tremendous size. The lips alone are about three feet wide.

to KV 5, the American Egyptologist Kent R. Weeks asked permission to try to locate the tomb.

By July, Weeks's crew was digging in the hard soil of the valley. After about ten days of work in the broiling sun, they came upon the entrance to KV 5. Weeks and his staff then began the staggering job of clearing out and exploring the tomb. It turned out to be the biggest tomb in the valley. So far, they have uncovered more than 110 separate rooms. And they are still digging.

Markings and carvings on the walls led Weeks and others to an interesting conclusion. Ramses II built this

tomb for his many sons, not for himself. He dug a separate tomb, KV 7, for his own burial. The site of KV 7, however, was not a good one; big sections have collapsed and the wall paintings have flaked off and been lost.

Explorers discovered the mummy of Ramses II in the same cache as the body of Thutmosis I. Although the bodies were all crammed together, most of the mummies were still in coffins with their names inscribed. Also, scattered around the cache were jars, scrolls, jewelry, and funeral offerings, which helped to identify the mummies.

Kent Weeks and a helper (left) are at work inside KV 5. Over the centuries, flash floods filled the tomb with mud and other debris. The plan (below) shows KV 5, which Ramses II had built for his more than 50 sons. Since the pharaoh lived to be very old, many of his children died before their father. The light-colored areas in the drawing have not yet been excavated but are expected to be the same as those already explored.

Using this evidence, scientists were able to identify Ramses II as well as many other pharaohs. One interesting detail came to light: Ramses II probably had red hair!

About 14 pharaohs were buried in the Valley of the Kings after Ramses II. Ramses X was the last. Why were future pharaohs buried elsewhere?

By the time of Ramses X, Egypt had lost much of its power in the ancient world. At home, priests, nobles, and army generals fought among themselves and divided Egypt into a number of smaller states. Outside Egypt, the many lands that had been conquered fought free of Egyptian rule. The pharaohs lost more and more of their authority.

As Egypt grew weaker, foreign leaders invaded and gained control of the country. They replaced the Egyptian kings. Neither the foreigners nor later Egyptians wanted to be buried in the Valley of the Kings. The New Kingdom was coming to an end. The sacred burial ground was abandoned.

The golden bracelet (above) belonged to Ramses II. Hinges with movable pins made it easy to slip on and off his wrist. According to the instructions of Ramses II, artists pictured his sons in a procession around the outside wall of his temple near the Valley of the Kings (right). Above the small figures of the boys sits the much larger pharaoh, facing Amon-Re, the sun god.

THE GREAT TOMB OF SETI I

Soon after Pharaoh Seti I took office in 1290 B.C. at age 26, he ordered Paser, his vizier or prime minister, to locate a spot in the Valley of the Kings for his tomb. After Seti approved the site, Paser went to the village of Deir el-Medina near the valley to direct the workers to dig the tomb. As vizier, Paser would oversee the construction.

The artists, stonecutters, wood carvers, and laborers who made the tombs lived in Deir el-Medina with their families. The men worked a 10-day week, eight days on the job and two days free. Since it was too far to walk from Deir el-Medina to the valley every day, the workers stayed in a small camp on the top of the cliff overlooking the valley during the work week and came home to their wives and children for weekends and holidays.

From the tomb of Seti I, a painting (above) illustrates warriors carrying the heads of their captives. Egyptologists found the well-preserved mummy of Seti I (right) in the cache at Deir El-Bahri.

Once the site for the tomb was chosen, Paser organized crews of stonecutters to carve out the tomb's many tunnels, passages, and rooms. With their sharp bronze chisels, the workmen chipped away, bit by bit, at the solid limestone cliff. As soon as they finished a section, other workers would arrive to plaster the walls and ceilings and ready them for decoration. Many of the paintings that adorned the tomb reflected the Egyptians' belief that Osiris, god of the underworld, would make the scenes come to life in the next world.

The workers who built the tombs in the valley lived in nearby Deir el-Medina (left). At home, they taught their trades to their sons, carved objects for the tombs, and traded the food they received as salary for other household supplies. Some craftsmen dug and decorated tombs for themselves (above). The decorations provide views of their modest lives—and their expectations for the afterlife.

BUILDING A TOMB FIT FOR A PHARAOH

With large wooden mallets and bronze chisels, the stonecutters hacked out steps, corridors, and rooms in the solid limestone cliffs. As many as 120 laborers chipped at the solid stone and hauled away heavy baskets of debris. To prepare a surface for decorations, workers covered the walls with a smooth coat of plaster.

After it dried, an artist, by the light of small oil lamps, made a sketch on the plaster in red. A master painter then corrected any mistakes in the drawing in black and added details. Following the artists's lines, a skilled artisan carved the drawing into the plaster. For the last step, a painter colored the art. When the decorations of the tomb were nearly done, laborers hauled in a big, heavy stone sarcophagus. It stood ready to hold the pharaoh's coffin and mummified body after he died.

One outstanding painting from Seti's tomb depicts the young, attractive pharaoh standing before Osiris. Next to him stands Horus, son of Osiris, who is shown with the head of a falcon. There is also a very striking astronomical ceiling with impressive views of the constellations.

On the walls and pillars of Seti's tomb the artists inscribed long sections of text from sacred books. Selections from the *Amduat* trace the sun's journey through the underworld after it sets on earth. From the *Litany of Re* are excerpts that praise the 75 different forms of the sun god. And from the *Book of Gates*, passages appear that refer to the 12 gates that divide the 12 hours of the night.

After six years of work, the workmen finished Seti's tomb. It proved to be the longest (400 feet), deepest (four staircases leading down), and most ornately painted tomb in the entire Valley of the Kings.

Pharaoh Seti I reigned for only five years after his tomb was completed. Word of his death at age 37 spread quickly. As priests who served the pharaoh started preparing the body for burial, the nation entered a long period of mourning.

Because the Egyptians believed that the dead lived on in the next world, they preserved the pharaoh's body so that he might rise again like the sun. To prevent Seti I's body from decaying, they immediately started to dry and embalm, or mummify, it, as they did for all pharaohs, their families, and wealthy nobles.

Paintings and sacred writings in hieroglyphs completely cover all the walls, ceilings, and pillars inside Seti I's tomb. The decorations contained prayers and formulas intended to serve but one purpose—to guide and protect the dead pharaoh on his journey to the underworld. No one thought they would be displayed and admired by future generations.

Before beginning the mummification process, the priests recited the special spells and prayers said on the death of a pharaoh. Embalmers then washed and anointed the royal corpse with oil. After that, they removed the stomach, lungs, intestines, and liver as a surgeon would. The organs were dried and placed into separate jars, called canopic jars. Then the embalmers used a long hook to pull the brain out through the nose. The heart remained in the body, since the Egyptians believed that this organ was the seat of the soul.

Next, the priests placed the body on a slanted bed and covered it, inside and out, with a salt called natron to remove all the moisture. Forty days later, they brushed away the natron from the dried corpse and filled the empty abdomen with linen or sawdust to restore its original shape. Finally, they wrapped the body carefully with narrow linen bandages, setting dozens of jewels and magical charms between the layers.

As the ancient texts instructed, the priests spent 70 days preparing the body for burial. While the embalmers were finishing, other workers fashioned Seti's coffins. Sometimes the men crafted two or three coffins that fit one inside the other.

In the funeral procession
(top), family, friends, and
servants carried the many objects the king would
need in the next world—a bed, chair, chests containing
clothing, sandals, a fan and walking stick, and much more. Mourners in
the procession shrieked, tore their clothes, and flung dust on their heads.
The priests put four of the pharaoh's organs into separate canopic jars like
the ones above. The stomach went into a jar with a jackal stopper, the
lungs into a baboon jar, intestines into a falcon-headed jar, and the liver
into a jar with a stopper shaped like a human head.

When all was ready, servants loaded the mummy in its coffins onto a boat and sailed to the king's temple on the west bank of the river. From there, a long, slow, mournful procession wound its way over the arid land to the Valley of the Kings.

Ramses II, the new pharaoh, along with high government and army officials, preceded the coffin of Seti drawn on a sledge by two oxen. A second sledge followed with the canopic jars. Family, friends, and servants carried the many objects that the dead king would need in the next world. Lines of masked and costumed priests and priestesses made up the rest of the funeral procession.

Once the mourners arrived at the tomb, the priests performed the final rituals before burial. These rites included the "opening of the mouth" ceremony.

According to Egyptian belief, the pharaoh's life force, or *ka*, left his body when he died. Mummification sealed his mouth and eyes shut; the *ka* could not re-enter. For rebirth to occur, the mummy's mouth and eyes had to be opened and its senses restored so the *ka* could return and the pharaoh could recite the prayers that would open the gates to the underworld. The priests held the mummy upright, while the high priest and the pharaoh's sons touched the mummy's face three times with various sacred objects to open the mouth and eyes and let the *ka* enter. Then they laid the dead king in his coffin and lowered it into the giant stone sarcophagus.

This drawing of the "opening of the mouth" ceremony comes from a book describing the rituals that must be performed before a pharaoh can enter the underworld. In this case, the jackal-headed god Anubis supports the mummy while priests conduct the ritual. Such books stayed with the mummy in his tomb to help him in the afterlife.

The mourners also set some 700 small statues, called *ushabtis*, in the tomb. These are undersized carvings of servants and field workers that, it was believed, would come to life and serve the ruler in the afterlife. All during the ceremony, the priests recited prayers and burned incense as part of the burial ritual.

Finally, stoneworkers sealed the tomb shut with a doorway of heavy rocks held together with cement. On the outside plaster, the priests put their seals and marked the name of the pharaoh buried within.

Seti's vast burial tomb was as safe from thieves as workers of the day could make it. Nevertheless, the tomb was robbed about 200 years after he was buried. And the thieves took nearly everything , although they left his well-preserved mummy in a magnificent marble sarcophagus in the tomb.

The Italian explorer Giovanni Belzoni discovered Seti's splendid—but empty—tomb in 1817. Years later, in 1881, Egyptologists found his mummy in the secret tomb outside the valley, the same tomb that held the mummies of Thutmosis I, Ramses II, and more than 40 other pharaohs.

The Valley of the Kings dates back over 3,500 years. But the pharaohs are very much alive to Egyptologists today. Every year, using the most advanced tools, from X-rays to DNA analysis, scientists add fascinating details to what is already known of the ancient rulers. New and exciting finds in the Valley of the Kings are sure to appear in the years to come.

Priests placed these small model figures of servants and farm workers, called **ushabtis**, in the pharaoh's tomb. The word *ushabtis*, means "answerers." The ancient Egyptians held that the *ushabtis* would come to life in the underworld and serve their master, "answering" for him whenever he was called on to perform a task. These **ushabtis** are all farm workers. They represent different periods and illustrate the changing styles over the years.

BIBLIOGRAPHY

Brier, Bob.
The Murder of Tutankhamen.
New York: Putnam, 1998.

Erman, Adolf.
Life in Ancient Egypt.
New York: Dover, 1971.

McMahan, Ian.
Secrets of the Pharaohs.
New York: Avon, 1998.

Reeves, Nicholas and
Richard H. Wilkinson.
The Complete Valley of the Kings. New
York: Thames and Hudson, 1996.

Reeves, Nicholas.
Into the Mummy's Tomb.
New York: Scholastic, 1992.

Silverman, David P., editor.
Ancient Egypt.
New York: Oxford University Press,
1997.

Web Site
WWW.KV5.com
For authoritative, up-to-date
information on KV 5 and other tombs
in the Valley of the Kings.

INDEX

The world's largest nonprofit
scientific and educational
organization, the National
Geographic Society was
founded in 1888 "for the
increase and diffusion of
geographic knowledge." Since
then it has supported scientific exploration and
spread information to its more than nine million
members worldwide. The National Geographic
Society educates and inspires millions every day
through magazines, books, television programs,
videos, maps and atlases, research grants, the
National Geographic Bee, teacher workshops,
and innovative classroom materials. The Society
is supported through membership dues and
income from the sale of its educational products.
For more information, please call 1-800-NGS-
LINE (647-5463) or visit the Society's Web site
at www.nationalgeographic.com